I0503293

Purpose

The purpose of this document is to provide information to investigators and prosecutors about the capabilities of the National Drug Intelligence Center (NDIC) Document and Media Exploitation (DOMEX) program, its methodology, its products, and how it can help the legal team with their investigations and prosecutions.

This guide is intended to help our customers prepare for the end result—use of products at trial to help secure convictions. This guide will help our customers develop their requests, think about the end state desired, and determine what analysis, information, and products are needed to support that end state. Spending a little time on the front end thinking about and developing goals will pay great dividends at trial.

Mission Statement

The National Drug Intelligence Center shall maintain the personnel and technical resources to provide timely support to law enforcement authorities and the intelligence community by conducting document and media exploitation of materials collected in federal, state, and local law enforcement activity associated with counterdrug, counterterrorism, and national security investigations and operations.

Document and Media Exploitation

NDIC's DOMEX methodology comprises the process of gleaning information from evidentiary material seized in connection with law enforcement investigations of counterdrug, counterterrorism, or national security investigations based on explicit search parameters established by the investigative team (investigators and prosecutors). The search parameters used in NDIC DOMEX missions are known as Priority Intelligence Requirements (PIRs).

NDIC has established a unique document and media exploitation program that has proved its effectiveness in approximately 1,000 investigations since 1993, including some of the highest-profile investigations in the United States. Upon execution of search warrants in many large cases, law enforcement officers often comment that they have too much data and not enough information. This is where the NDIC capability is instrumental; turning raw data into actionable information is our highest priority. Keys to our success include our trained Intelligence Analysts (IAs), who work full-time on DOMEX missions; an application called the Real-time Analytical Intelligence Database (RAID); and our Digital Evidence Laboratory Information Technology Specialists (ITSs), who are highly skilled in digital evidence exploitation.

Completeness of Evidence

The document and media exploitation service that we provide, as well as any follow-on testimonial support, is greatly impacted by the quality of the evidence our customers provide. Receiving an incomplete evidence package, or copies of evidence rather than original documents or digital media, may impact our ability to provide a complete intelligence report or detailed trial testimony. In order to provide the highest-quality reports and testimony, we must receive the best available evidence from our customers.

Priority Intelligence Requirements (PIRs)

PIRs are specific search parameters established and approved by the investigative team that guide DOMEX personnel during their review and analysis of the electronic and paper evidence, the identification of which will further the investigation or assist in the prosecution of the suspects. Examples of PIRs include, but are not limited to, the identification of associates, assets, addresses, telephone numbers, events, and indications of money laundering or other criminal activity. PIRs vary from mission to mission depending on the objectives of the investigative team and type of evidence analyzed. The development of PIRs tailored to the objectives of the investigation is crucial to the successful completion of each DOMEX mission. Therefore, it is crucial that the legal team work closely with NDIC DOMEX personnel to identify, develop, and tailor PIRs to meet the needs of investigators and prosecutors in a timely manner.

DOMEX Process

The DOMEX process begins when a customer submits a formal written request to NDIC asking for DOMEX support. Once we receive the request, an assessment is conducted to determine the level of support needed.

The assessment involves NDIC DOMEX personnel as well as investigators and, sometimes, prosecutors. It is conducted via telephone, although in some cases we may travel to the field office to meet with the Assistant U.S. Attorney (AUSA) and/or the case investigators. Before analyzing any evidence, we spend time with the case agents and/or prosecutors to determine what information is needed to move the case forward. We establish PIRs after careful evaluation of the requestor's needs and the type and quantity of evidence.

The following are examples of PIRs that we've used in past cases:

- Information pertaining to a subject and his associates
- Financial transactions exceeding a specified amount
- Phone numbers in a particular city, state, or country
- References to a specific crime in notes, e-mails, or other communications
- Any unknown assets of the target and his associates

PIRs vary from mission to mission; however, identifying assets is the PIR common to all cases. Asset forfeiture is one of our top priorities.

If the request for assistance is approved, NDIC forms a DOMEX team usually consisting of 15 to 20 analysts chosen for their subject matter expertise, and if necessary, language ability.

Our DOMEX teams can produce and deliver a final product within approximately 2–3 weeks. However, cases that include large amounts of evidence may take longer. Regardless of mission size, NDIC DOMEX personnel provide regular updates to requestors regarding the progress of a mission. If time-sensitive information is uncovered, we attempt to notify investigatory personnel in order to maximize the benefit that may be achieved by acting upon such information.

In addition to our main office in Johnstown, Pennsylvania, we have satellite DOMEX units at the following locations:

- The headquarters of the **Utah National Guard/Joint Language Training Center** (JLTC) in Riverton, Utah. NDIC partnered with the Utah National Guard to establish a DOMEX team whereby their linguistic personnel are thoroughly trained in the use of RAID and our DOMEX methodology. This NDIC DOMEX team is led by a senior NDIC IA, and it principally works on our DOMEX missions that consist of significant amounts of foreign language material.

- **Organized Crime Drug Enforcement Task Force (OCDETF) Strike Force locations.** NDIC partnered with the OCDETF and its Asset Forfeiture program to establish DOMEX teams in five locations supporting OCDETF Strike Force and SWB operations. Our use of these locations has expanded our scope of support into the field. The **Atlanta** team became operational on April 27, 2009. The **Houston** team became operational on June 8, 2009. In the spring of 2010, three more teams were established in **San Diego**, **El Paso**, and **Phoenix**. These teams are solely dedicated to supporting the OCDETF Strike Force investigations in those regions.

We have teams of highly trained and experienced DOMEX analysts who have worked many different cases over the years. We are able to turn lessons learned on one investigation into valuable experience that can be applied to future DOMEX missions. We have developed a unique expertise on how to glean information from documentary and electronic media data and how to capture it in a way that promotes analysis and visual representation of that data for the benefit of both the investigation and the prosecution.

Digital Evidence Laboratory

Almost every investigation that we support has a digital data storage component, which includes the exploitation of computers, PDAs, BlackBerries, cell phones, and digital cameras. To exploit the information contained in these devices, we engage the capabilities of our Digital Evidence Laboratory (DEL). The electronic media exploitation conducted by our DEL personnel has proved to be an extremely valuable component of our program.

Digital evidence exploitation, like document and media exploitation, also uses PIRs to guide the analysis. The DEL examiners follow the same PIRs that DOMEX analysts use to exploit evidence. All information found by DEL examiners is delivered to the DOMEX team for analysis in combination with the documentary evidence.

Real-time Analytical Intelligence Database (RAID)

RAID is the primary application tool used by our DOMEX teams to provide actionable investigative intelligence to our customers on counterdrug, counterterrorism, and national security investigations. For example, our analysts used RAID in support of the World Trade Center and Pentagon bombing investigations. Users working in a networked environment can share information gleaned during document exploitation activities on a real-time basis or manage case intelligence information during an investigation. RAID's point-and-click ease of use, powerful relational capabilities, and compatibility with other software make organization and analysis of information extremely flexible and manageable.

The RAID application was created at NDIC in 1995 using Microsoft Access and has evolved into a robust tool capable of exporting data into powerful, commercially available analytical software. RAID was developed by analysts for analysts to provide better intelligence and data support in large investigations. The application helps specialists catalog and analyze valuable information gleaned from seized evidence, Reports of Investigation, subpoenaed information, electronic media, and other intelligence sources. The RAID application allows the creation and linking of data in a distributed environment. This means that records created by one analyst are instantly available to other analysts, and updates are seen in real time. Data contained in RAID can also be displayed visually using commercially available analytical software such as i2 Analyst's Notebook and Geographic Information Systems (GISs) such as ArcView.

RAID is a multiuser relational database management system used by NDIC as well as other intelligence and law enforcement agencies. In fact, more than 4,000 copies of the application have been distributed to agencies in both domestic and international locations. RAID operates with Microsoft's full SQL Server platform. This ensures that we can provide a copy of our database to any agency we support without requiring additional software. RAID has been upgraded to a new .NET Framework as well as SQL Server 2008 and SQL Server Express.

A list and brief description of the principal forms, as well as some of the features, available in RAID appear on page 19.

RAID Certification and Accreditation

The RAID application has been certified and accredited. The Certification and Accreditation (C&A) process establishes a standard security baseline across a specified information system. A C&A is required for all reportable information systems and major applications by the Federal Information Security Act of 2001 and is mandated by the U.S. Department of Justice, Office of the Chief Information Officer. The C&A assessment activities attempt to do the following: describe the system or major application, identify threats and vulnerabilities, select the appropriate controls for that system, implement those controls and assess control performance, conduct a risk assessment, mitigate risks, and monitor change management.

The ultimate goal of a C&A is to maintain the confidentiality, integrity, and availability of an information system or major application while facilitating operations.

Evidence Types

During our DOMEX process, we have the ability to exploit several types of evidence, including the following:

- Evidence obtained by operation of a search warrant or consent to search
- Subpoenaed financial records
- Electronic evidence such as computers, cell phones, and PDAs
- E-mails
- Prescriptions—electronic or hard copy
- Patient files
- Reports of Investigation

Mission Types

Our DOMEX teams are flexible and can adapt to diverse investigations. DOMEX analysts come from a variety of backgrounds, have been trained in the use of powerful analytical tools, and many possess 15-plus years' experience.

The following are types of investigations we have supported:

- Child Exploitation
- Counterdrug
- National Security
- Terrorism
- Gangs
- Health Care Fraud
- Internet Pharmacies
- Kidnapping
- Marijuana Grow Houses
- Money Laundering
- Pharmaceutical Diversion
- Political Corruption
- Steroids

Final Products

To gain the full value and benefit of our analysis, NDIC uses a variety of analytical tools, resulting in informative and comprehensive final products. Typical final products include the following:

The **RAID Report** is the database that is provided to the requestor in both hard and soft copy. It contains all the intelligence derived from the evidence, with every piece of information sourced back to the original evidence. Each RAID Report is made up of seven different types of Main Subject Areas (MSAs). These MSAs include Account, Address, Biographical, Event, Item,

Telephone, and Vehicle. Each MSA is cross-referenced with others to which connections and relationships were found.

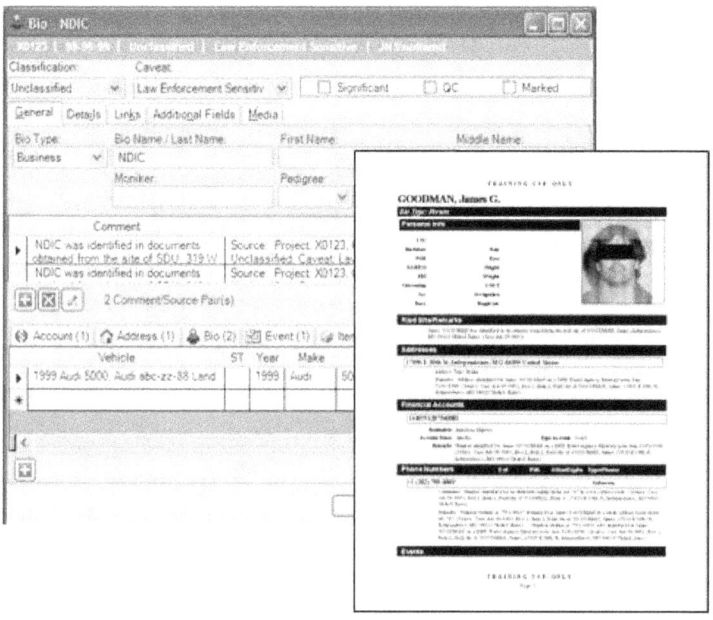

Figure 1. A Bio MSA As It Appears in the RAID Application and As Printed in a RAID Report

The **Intelligence Support Report** (ISR) is a narrative written by the lead analyst and his or her team analysts. It contains all of the team's findings that directly meet the PIRs for the mission and any additional information that could further the investigation.

DOMEX also provides **additional products** to customers, such as maps, time lines, link charts, spreadsheets, and pivot tables, as required. Information can be easily understood and communicated visually with i2 charts, graphs, and GIS maps. All the information contained in our reports and products is supported by and sourced back to the original evidence, whether a document or an electronic file. Since we work closely with our customers, the products we generate can be tailored to meet their needs.

The following are examples of final products developed for our customers:

ASSOCIATION LINKS
IDENTIFIED IN FBI CASE NUMBER -

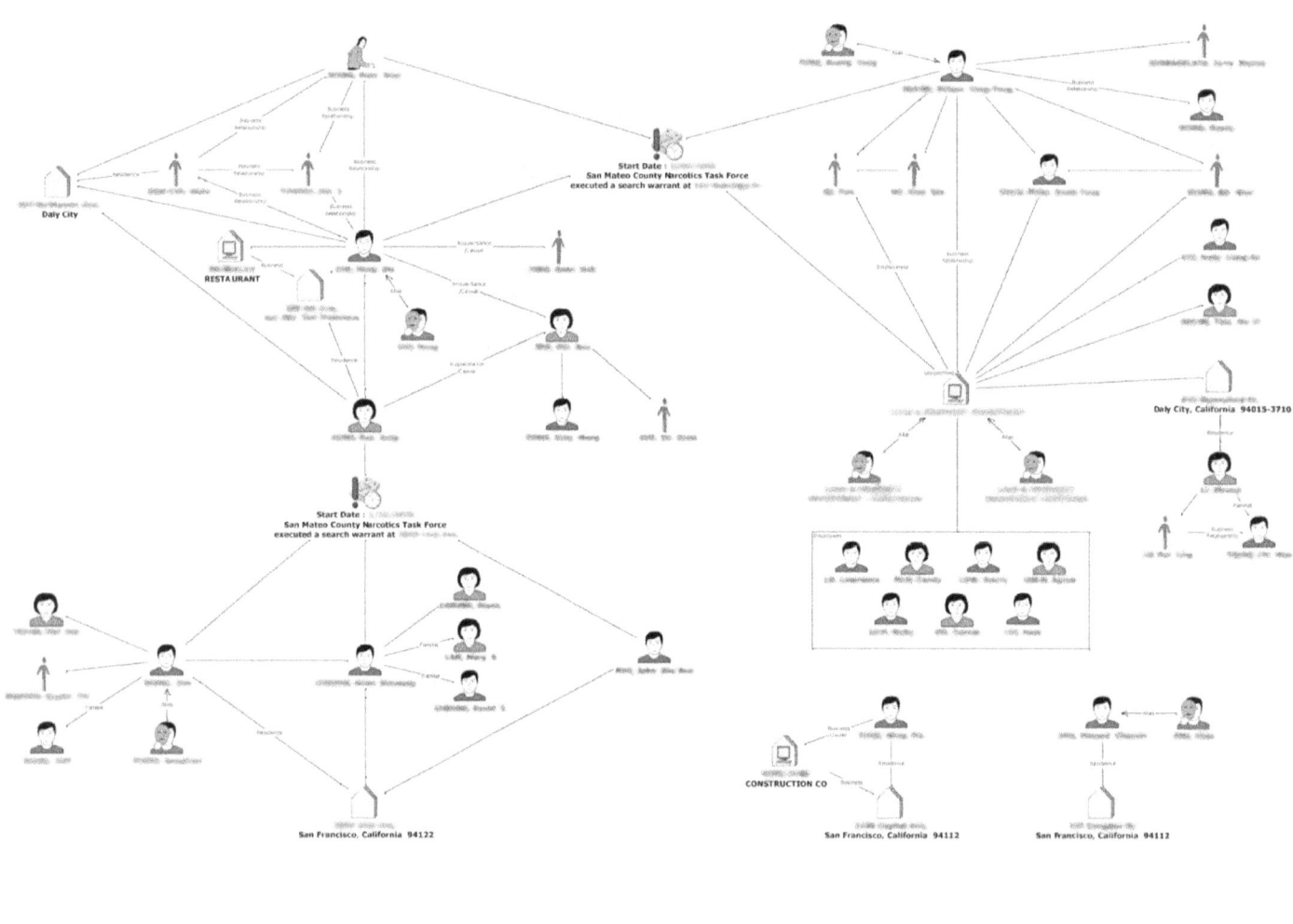

This chart contains information for intelligence
purposes. Information contained within this chart
should be verified from primary source information
before action is taken.
THIS PRODUCT IS A PRELIMINARY PRODUCT

Figure 2. Association Chart

*This is an example of a link chart created from the information entered in RAID. This link chart
provides a visual representation of associates, addresses, telephones, vehicles, financial
accounts, and items related to the main target of this investigation. In addition, it shows aliases
and personal identifiers such as passport and driver's license numbers.*

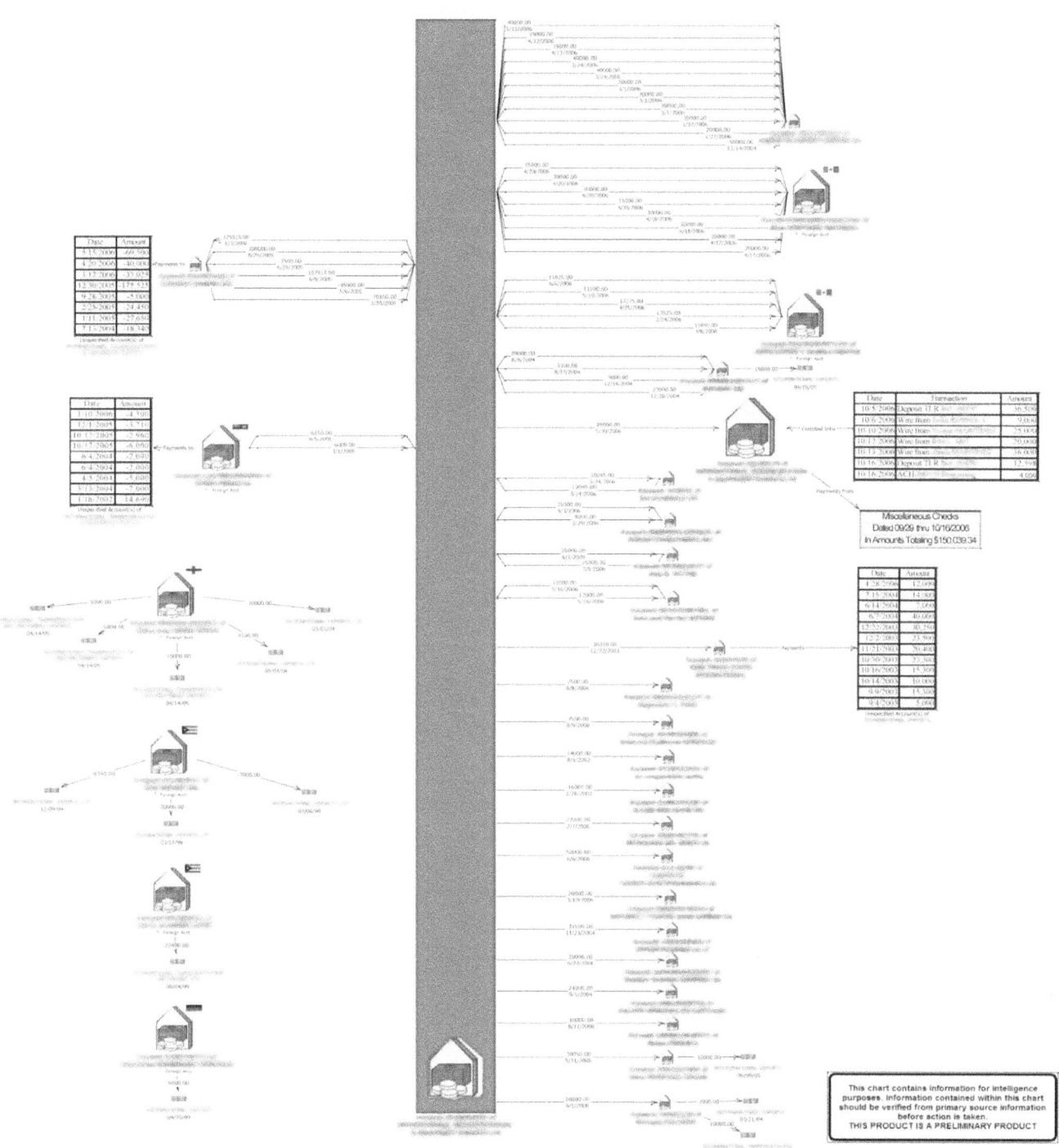

Figure 3. Financial Flow Chart

This chart depicts the financial flow of an organization. The data for this chart were obtained from subpoenaed financial information.

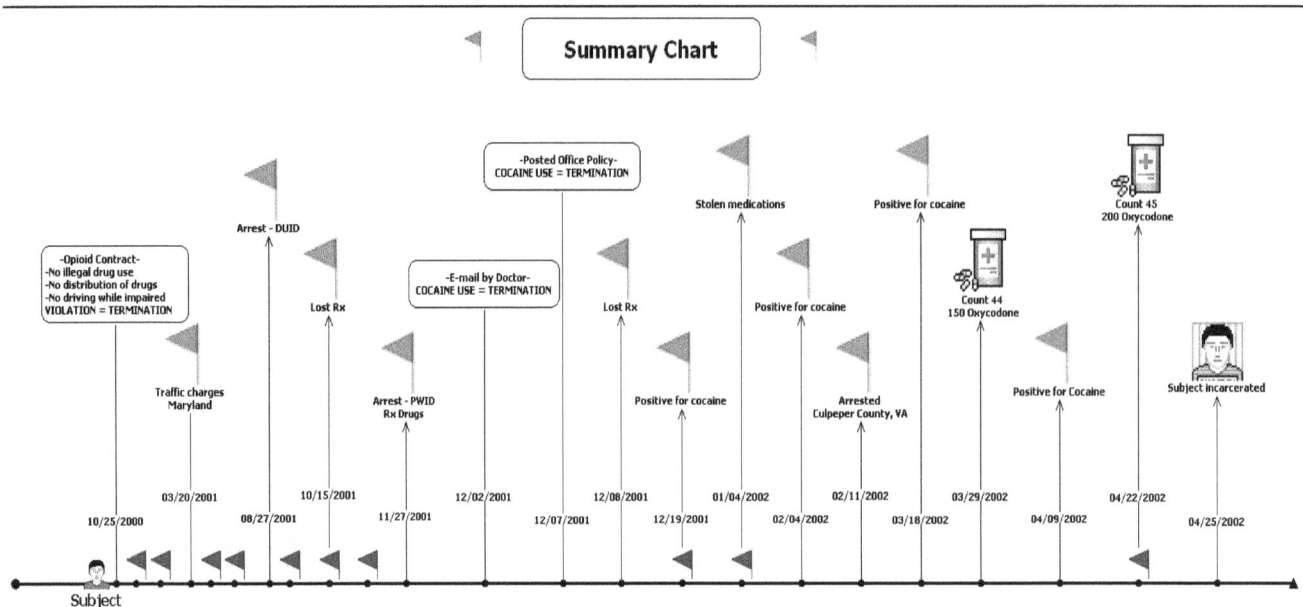

Figure 4. Event Chart

In diversion investigations, a time line can be created from a patient file and Reports of Investigation to document a patient's history.

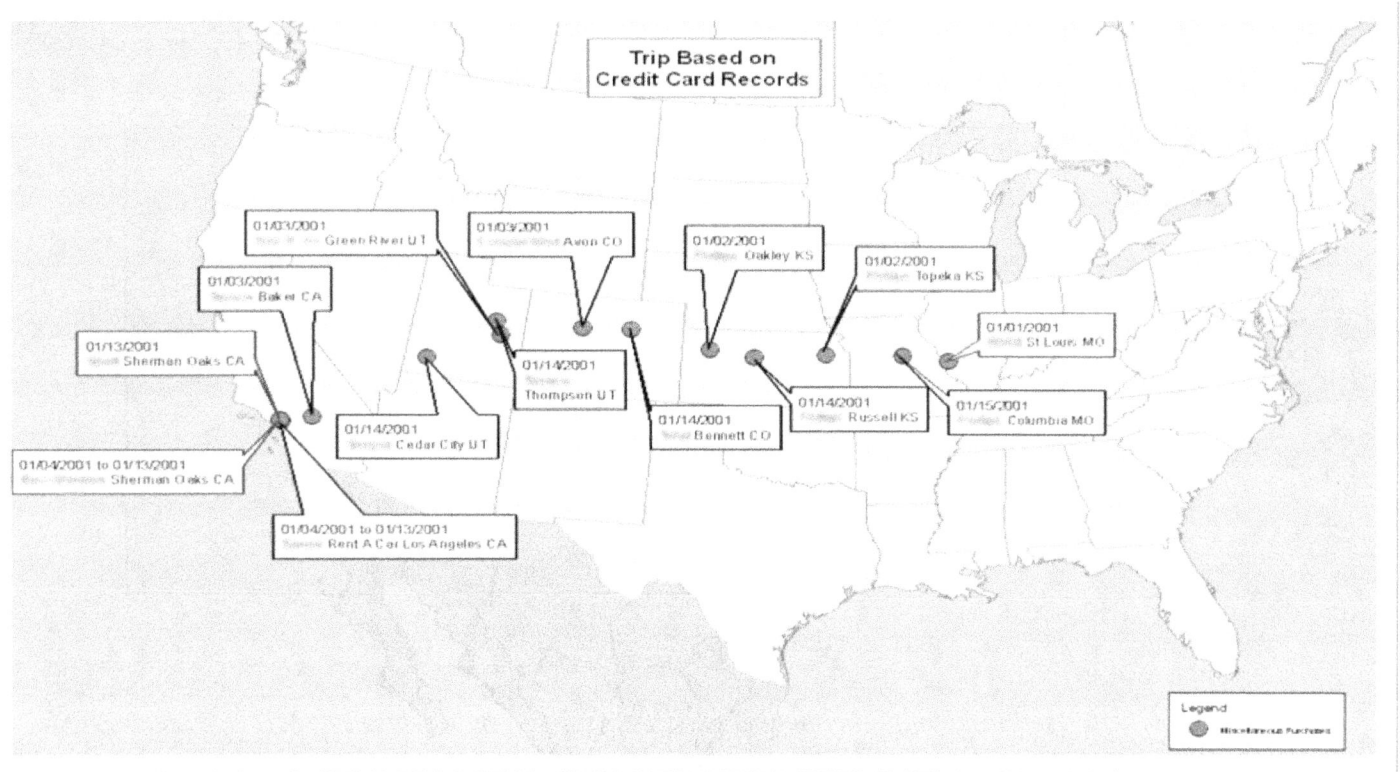

Figure 5. GIS Map Depicting a Subject's Travel Based on Sales Receipts and Credit Card Statements That Were Found in the Evidentiary Material

This is an example of GIS mapping based on locations identified on receipts and credit card statements. Because the time, date, and location of transactions were documented, the target was tracked across the country and was proved to be in a certain location at a certain time.

Row Labels	Count of RX
SMITH, John	7,913
Benzodiazepine	1,773
Narcotic	5,983
Other	157
Grand Total	7,913

Figure 6. Pivot Table

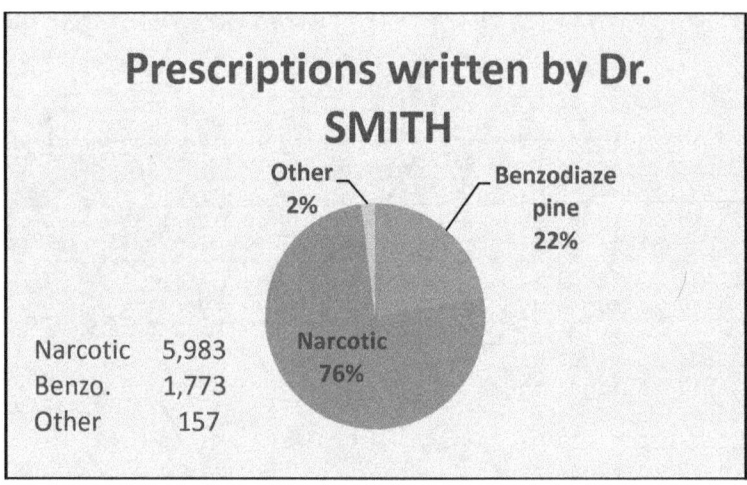

Figure 7. Pie Chart Based on Figure 6 Pivot Table

A pivot table was used to identify the number of prescriptions written by Dr. SMITH. A second criterion was added to the pivot table to break down the prescriptions into one of three categories: Benzodiazepine, Narcotic, and Other. A pie chart was produced from the results of the pivot table to show the percentage of prescriptions written for narcotics and benzodiazepines versus all other types of medication.

Requesting DOMEX Support or RAID Application

Customers wishing to obtain DOMEX support and/or a RAID application must submit a formal written request to NDIC. Requests should be submitted on agency letterhead and signed by an appropriate senior-level official. Please see page 22 to view a sample request letter for DOMEX support. See page 23 to view a RAID application request form.

Legal and Litigation Issues

Search Warrants and Authorizations

The case agent/prosecutor should forward copies of all search warrants, search authorizations, and consent-to-search documents to NDIC in preparation for the DOMEX mission.[1] NDIC personnel sometimes discover evidence/indications of crimes outside the scope of the warrant/authorization/consent. Upon discovery, we normally suspend work on that portion of the evidence and provide information to the case agent/prosecutor for guidance. We provide affidavits in support of additional search warrant/authorization applications, as appropriate.

Child Pornography

NDIC DEL examiners uncover known or suspected child pornography in DOMEX cases with some frequency. As stated above, NDIC DEL personnel who uncover known or suspected child pornography will suspend the examination and notify the case agent/prosecutor of the existence of such evidence.

Grand Jury Secrecy: Federal Rules of Criminal Procedure 6(e)

NDIC routinely handles 6(e) materials. We have a well-established evidence-tracking system, evidence vaults, and dedicated evidence-tracking personnel. NDIC maintains a list of personnel who may have access to 6(e) materials. Although this list is larger than many comparable 6(e) lists, it provides maximum flexibility to NDIC and facilitates the rapid processing of DOMEX missions. The employees on NDIC's 6(e) list are aware of their responsibilities regarding 6(e) materials. Agents and prosecutors can be confident that NDIC employees will handle all the evidence provided to them in accordance with Rule 6(e) requirements.

Attorney-Client Information and Taint Team Issues

We request the names and identifying information of all known defense attorneys or any other attorney who may have entered into an attorney-client relationship with persons included in the evidence in a particular DOMEX mission. NDIC DEL examiners can segregate any suspected attorney-client privileged information and provide a sanitized set of materials to the DOMEX team. If such evidence is discovered, NDIC will notify the case agent/prosecutor of its existence. Based upon the guidance we receive from the case agent/prosecutor, NDIC can either implement its own taint team process or return suspected attorney-client privileged material to the case agent/prosecutor for evaluation by a taint team in his or her respective district.

---

[1] In light of the Ninth Circuit Court of Appeals decision in *U.S. v. Comprehensive Drug Testing, Inc.,* 579 F.3d 989 (9th Cir.2009), it is imperative that NDIC receive any warrant that cites to or contains additional "CDT protocols."

Testimony of NDIC DOMEX Personnel

NDIC DOMEX personnel are frequently called to testify at trials. Intelligence Analysts are generally called to testify regarding the exploitation of documents, the information gleaned from pharmacy records, or the production of charts and graphs depicting our analysis. DEL examiners are most often called to testify regarding their forensic examination of electronic evidence. Travel and temporary duty (TDY) costs are borne by the requesting prosecutor's office.

In situations where NDIC DEL examinations have resulted in findings having no apparent probative value, yet defense counsel intends to subpoena the examiner to testify, the prosecutor should inform defense counsel of NDIC's policy requiring payment of the examiner's travel expenses by defense counsel. We recommend that in such cases prosecutors attempt to secure a stipulation concerning this testimony to avoid needless expenditures of time and money attendant to the examiner's appearance in court.

Discovery – Fed. R. Crim. P. 16 and FRCP 26 – DOMEX/RAID Materials

It is the responsibility of the lead counsel on any prosecution team to determine the discovery obligations in their cases. It is not appropriate for NDIC to advise or opine regarding the discovery obligations in a particular case or a specific district. Prosecutors may wish to seek review *in limine* in appropriate cases. Prosecutors may also need to secure a protective order in cases where the DOMEX data/RAID database contains Personally Identifiable Information (PII) or similar data not suitable for release to criminal defendants.

If you are planning to call an NDIC DOMEX analyst to testify as an expert, additional discovery may be warranted under FRCP 26(a)(2). Upon request, NDIC will produce draft trial exhibits for disclosure to the defense in discovery. Final versions will be provided shortly before trial. See also **Modification of NDIC Products**, *below*.

Disclosure of Exculpatory—*Brady* Material

It is the responsibility of the lead counsel on any prosecution team to determine what information may require disclosure under *Brady v. Maryland*, 373 U.S. 83 (1963). NDIC adheres to the procedures outlined in the *United States Attorneys' Manual*, 9-5.001, "Policy Regarding Disclosure of Exculpatory and Impeachment Information." While we are not in a position to make *Brady* determinations, we can assist in identifying *Brady* material. If there are specific *Brady* concerns, they may be addressed during the PIR development process. Should we identify any *Brady* material during the course of the DOMEX mission, we will highlight those elements of information. The timing of *Brady* disclosures is the responsibility of the lead prosecutor.

Impeachment Evidence—*Giglio* Policy

Under *Giglio v. United States*, 405 U.S. 150 (1972), investigative agencies must turn over to prosecutors, as early as possible in a case, potential impeachment evidence with respect to government witnesses who will testify at trial. NDIC personnel called as witnesses are responsible for informing the prosecution team of any potential *Giglio* issues. NDIC follows the guidance outlined in the *United States Attorney Manual*, 9-5.100, "Policy Regarding the Disclosure to Prosecutors of Potential Impeachment Information Concerning Law Enforcement Agency Witnesses ('Giglio Policy')." As with *Brady* material, it is the responsibility of the lead prosecutor to exercise his or her discretion as to whether any potential impeachment evidence must be turned over to the defense.

Jencks Act and Federal Rules of Criminal Procedure 26.2

The Jencks Act, 18 U.S.C. § 3500, provides that the government must produce a verbatim statement or report made by a government witness or prospective government witness (other than the defendant) after the witness has testified. Jencks material is evidence that is used in the course of a federal criminal prosecution in the United States. It usually consists of documents relied upon by government witnesses who testify at trial. It is described as *inculpatory*, favoring the U.S. Government's prosecution of a criminal defendant. The act also covers other documents related to the testimony or relied upon by government witnesses at trial, such as police notes, memoranda, reports, summaries, letters, or verbatim transcripts used by government agents or employees to testify at trial.

As with *Brady* and *Giglio*, it is the responsibility of the lead prosecutor to exercise his or her discretion as to whether any DOMEX materials constitute Jencks Act/FRCP 26.2 materials. The line between the trial exhibits produced through the DOMEX process and potential *Brady*, *Giglio*, or *Jencks* material may be difficult to discern. NDIC will not object to the prosecution's turning over any or all of a particular DOMEX report to the defense in a particular case. The following issues of concern should be addressed before a DOMEX product/RAID database is turned over to nongovernmental entities:

- Consult with the NDIC DOMEX lead analyst regarding specific modifications of DOMEX products/reports to reduce the information provided to only that which is necessary to meet discovery/disclosure needs.

- Secure a protective order for protection of Personally Identifiable Information (PII) contained in DOMEX products or RAID databases.

Admissibility of DOMEX Products

Admissibility issues relating to DOMEX products have arisen primarily in two contexts—uncharged misconduct and summary evidence. There is generally little case law regarding NDIC's DOMEX process; however, one Circuit Court opinion on the use of DOMEX in the Fed. R. Evid. 404(b) context is particularly helpful.

On January 17, 2008, the Eleventh Circuit Court affirmed Dr. Thomas Merrill's convictions for 98 of 100 counts of wire fraud, healthcare fraud, and the illegal prescribing of narcotics. Dr. Merrill's sentencing included life imprisonment on 6 counts and various concurrent sentences on 92 counts. Among the issues Merrill raised on appeal was an allegation that the trial court had abused its discretion when it allowed the government to introduce, through an NDIC Intelligence Analyst's testimony, a summary of the more than 33,000 prescriptions for controlled substances that Merrill had written between January 2001 and May 2004. The court found that the testimony and the summary were both properly admitted and relevant under Fed. R. Evid. 401-403 and did not violate Fed. R. Evid. 404(b). *U.S. v. Merrill*, 513 F.3d 1293 (11th Cir 2008).

The other area of concern has been Fed. R. Evid. 1006 summary or compilation evidence. To date we have no case law on point.

Modification of NDIC Products

We strongly recommend that case agents/prosecutors do not modify NDIC products intended for trial exhibits without the consent or knowledge of NDIC. Should you need to alter a product that will be used as an exhibit, please contact the lead analyst. He or she can make modifications, create new products, or suggest alternative products to meet the customer's needs. This will ensure that when NDIC analysts take the stand, their testimony will be based on products they have seen, are familiar with, and can authenticate.

Appendix

RAID Principal Forms

Inventory Record—The Inventory form is used to capture the location of the information source. It catalogs the Evidence or Report of Investigation (ROI) and therefore makes it easier to retrieve the evidence or document. The Inventory form contains raw source data such as the evidence, box, and item numbers.

Biographical MSA Record—The Biographical (Bio) form is used to track information relating to a person, business, organization, or gang; to identify relationships; and to create links to those entities. The Bio form is the most comprehensive MSA form. It allows users to make links to all other MSAs in RAID.

Address MSA Record—The Address form is used to track information relating to a location (physical mailing address, virtual e-mail or web site address, or geographical location [GPS, latitude/longitude] address), to identify relationships, and to create links to other MSA records in RAID.

Telephone MSA Record—The Phone MSA form is used to record and track information regarding telephone numbers and their association with other MSA records, including other Phone records. The import wizard allows RAID users to convert electronic copies of telephone transactions into individual link records for every telephone contact between Phone records.

Financial MSA Record—The Account MSA is used to record and track information regarding a financial account and the flow of assets between financial accounts. It handles all international monetary units.

Vehicle MSA Record—The Vehicle form is used to record and track information related to land vehicles, watercraft, and aircraft and to identify relationships and create links to those vehicles.

Events MSA Record—The Event MSA is used to record and track information relating to an action or occurrence that can be identified by some form of date.

Items MSA Record—The Item MSA is used to record and track information related to physical evidence such as art, documents, weapons, explosive components, fingerprints, and DNA.

RAID Features

Bookmarks—RAID gives users the ability to bookmark any of the MSA types and groups them accordingly.

Dynamic Additional Fields—In some instances, a mission might have special requirements that necessitate the collection of specific data. The Additional Fields feature for MSAs is used for such data. Each MSA type can have its own additional (custom) fields. Any user with full administrative access to a project can create these fields to supplement the standard fields that exist for an MSA.

Advanced Query Control—RAID's Advanced Query feature can be used to "filter," or find data by creating a custom query. The query can be as simple or as complex as needed in order to return only the records desired. This query control greatly facilitates analysis of sets of records within the database. The Advanced Query function in datasheet view has been enhanced to handle some of the same duplicate-type queries that previously were possible only in the Advanced Query Wizard on the toolbar.

Analyst Notebook Interface—The i2 Analyst's Notebook application (ANB) is visualization software used for accumulating, analyzing, and displaying complex relationships. It is used extensively by law enforcement agencies to define and visualize the links between pieces of evidence obtained during the course of an investigation. RAID integrates seamlessly with ANB. The user is able to view the data stored within the RAID database with the ANB visualization tool, enabling effective link and time-line analysis. RAID also allows each user to customize what data are transferred to i2 for biographical and financial information for labels, descriptions, and attributes.

Import/Export Wizard—RAID users can import and export records into and from the database using the Import/Export Wizards. The wizards guide users through the operations. When exporting data from the RAID system, the user invokes the Export Wizard, designates the file format, specifies the records to be exported, and specifies the name of the final export file. This is the feature used to export data into a format that can later be used in systems such as GIS. Likewise, when importing data, the user invokes the Import Wizard, designates the file format and the import file, and specifies the records to be created from the import file. RAID allows for the merging of duplicate records during imports. The upgrade in the newer .NET Framework has given the import/export wizards much greater power. Users can import thousands of rows of information at a time.

Robust Multimedia Capability—Assorted electronic files may be part of the evidence in a case. Any file type can be stored in RAID for later retrieval. Documents, spreadsheets, Adobe PDF files, graphic files, and more can all be catalogued within RAID. After a multimedia file has been associated with a project, it can then be associated with any Inventory record or MSA in the project. This enables the user to review the source of the information extracted and entered into RAID.

Adding Bios or Accounts from a Transaction—RAID gives users the ability to create a Bio or an Account from the Payor/Payee and Related Account sections of the Transaction screen. This enables users to save time by creating their Bio or Account on the fly rather than stopping to save and enter the MSAs separately.

Navigation Bars—RAID has navigation bars on the Datasheet view and QC Links views. This enables users to know that they are on record 29 of 289 or to quickly jump to record 140.

Sample DOMEX Mission Request Letter

Agency Letterhead
Agency Address

Insert Date

Mr. Harry J. Kuerner
Chief, Document and Media Exploitation Branch
National Drug Intelligence Center
319 Washington Street, 5th Floor
Johnstown, PA 15901-1622

Dear Mr. Kuerner:

The purpose of this letter is to request that the National Drug Intelligence Center's Document and Media Exploitation Branch provide analytical support to the *(insert your agency)*, *(insert your city)* Division, in case number *(insert your agency's case number and file title)* and OCDETF Operation *(name)* and OCDETF investigation number *(XX-SSS-1234)*. *(Insert information about why this case is significant [OCDETF, CPOT, SOD-coordinated, etc.,] and describe its regional/national/international impact.)* This investigation was initiated in *(insert month/year)* and worked in conjunction with *(insert other agencies, e.g., DEA, FBI, ATF, ICE, HIDTA, state, local, if applicable)*.

(Background/history of case—Include type and quantity of drugs involved; gang involvement; violence; organized crime; maritime, air, or vehicular smuggling routes; international/domestic; any assets that have been seized or identified thus far; any evidence of money laundering or corruption.)

(Current status of the case—Include the number of arrests or indictments, geographic locations, number of search warrants, type and volume of seized evidence; type of container where the evidence was found (e.g., three-drawer filing cabinet, five hard drives, multiple CDs/DVDs, four Xerox boxes), including travel records, money orders, shipping records, financial transactions, telephone information, utility bills, passports, computer or electrical evidence of seized documents, business records, and type of business. If your seized items include digital media (including e-mails), will you require any computer or media exploitation? If so, you will need to provide search authority or the subpoena for the items.)

(Include a list/accounting of those services you would like us to provide to you. This information will help us complete our assessment of your request and frame suitable PIRs. Examples include:

- *Identification of assets, including evidence of money laundering, sources of supply, and analysis of financial documents*
- *Identification of associates, including addresses and telephone numbers)*

(Insert points of contact/case agent, supervisor, AUSA names, and telephone numbers.)

Sincerely,
Name
Duty Position/Title

((Agency Letterhead))

Date

RAID Request
National Drug Intelligence Center
319 Washington St., 5th Floor
Johnstown, PA 15901-1622

This letter requests a copy of the National Drug Intelligence Center's Real-time Analytical Intelligence Database (RAID) application. All sections of this letter must be completed.

SECTION I: Your Agency Information

Agency Name: _____

Federal: ☐   State: ☐   Local: ☐   International: ☐   Other: ☐   Tribal: ☐

Requester Name (First, MI, Last): _____

☐ Mr.   ☐ Mrs.   ☐ Ms.   ☐ Title: _____

Address: _____

City: _____

State/Country: _____   Zip: _____

Phone Number(s):   Work: (__) (____) ____ - _____ ext: _____

Fax: (__) (____) ____ - _____

Email Address: _____

Technical Point-of-Contact (If other than requester)

Name (First, MI, Last): _____

☐ Mr.   ☐ Mrs.   ☐ Ms.   ☐ Title: _____

Address: _____

City: _____

State/Country: _____   Zip: _____

Phone Number(s):   Work: (__) (____) ____ - _____ ext: _____

Fax: (__) (____) ____ - _____

Email Address: _____

2nd Technical Point-of-Contact (optional)

Name (First, MI, Last): _____

☐ Mr.   ☐ Mrs.   ☐ Ms.   ☐ Title: _____

Address: _____

City: _____

State/Country: _____   Zip: _____

Phone Number(s):   Work: (__) (____) ____ - _____ ext: _____

Fax: (__) (____) ____ - _____

Email Address: _____

RAID will be used to: ☐ Analyze seized evidence
                               ☐ Manage ongoing case information
                               ☐ Other _____

Has this agency used an earlier version of RAID?
            ☐ No
            ☐ Yes, version(s) _____.
            Will you import the current data into the RAID database?
            ☐ Yes   ☐ No

Describe the type of investigations RAID will support: _____
_____

If you already have a copy of RAID, how did you receive your copy?
            ☐ NDIC Document Exploitation Mission, Date: _____
            ☐ Trade Show, Name of Trade Show & Date: _____
            ☐ Other, Please describe: _____

Has this agency received a RAID Training Class?
            ☐ No
            ☐ Yes,   date(s): _____ for version(s) _____

Do you request training for RAID?
            ☐ No   ☐ Yes

Note: NDIC would like to support all requests for training in the use of the RAID application by members of the law enforcement and intelligence communities. However, budget and resource constraints require that NDIC limit training to only those agencies or offices that pay or agree to share information. By accepting RAID training, your agency or office agrees to reimburse NDIC for all costs associated with training or provide NDIC with either a copy of the databases created using the RAID application or with synopses of the cases supported using the RAID application. These synopses can be general, but should contain sufficient information to enable the information to be used to support strategic assessments prepared by NDIC. If you agree to share

RAID data or case synopses with NDIC, please sign the enclosed Information Sharing Agreement.

SECTION II: RAID License Packaging and Hardware Requirements

Standalone Environment

The standalone environment consists of one configuration that includes one desktop or laptop computer, the RAID system application, and SQL Express 2008 database software that serves as the RAID system database. RAID operates autonomously in this environment. The following is a summary of the hardware requirements when operating in a standalone environment. Please refer to the Installation Guide for additional details and caveats.

Component	Requirement
32-bit Standalone Computers	
Processor	Processor Type: • Pentium III-compatible processor or faster Processor Speed: • Minimum: 1.0 GHz • Recommended: 2.0 GHz or faster
Operating System	Windows XP SP2 Professional Windows Server 2003 SP2 Standard Windows Vista Enterprise Windows Server 2008 Standard Server Windows 7 Professional
Memory	RAM: • Minimum: 512 MB for SQL Server Express with Tools, and SQL Server Express with Advanced Services • Recommended: 1.024 GB • Maximum: 1 GB for the Database Engine that installs with SQL Server Express, SQL Server Express with Tools, and SQL Server Express with Advanced Services, 4 GB for Reporting Services that installs with SQL Server Express with Advanced Services Disk: 1-5 GB, depending on software configuration
64-bit Standalone Computers	
Processor	Processor Type: • Minimum: AMD Opteron, AMD Athlon 64, Intel Xeon with Intel EM64T support, Intel Pentium IV with EM64T support Processor Speed: • Minimum: 1.4 GHz • Recommended: 2.0 GHz or faster
Operating System	Windows Server 2003 SP2 64-bit x64 Standard Windows Vista Enterprise 64-bit x64 Windows Server 2008 64-bit x64 Standard Windows 7 64-bit x64 Professional
Memory	RAM: • Minimum: 512 MB • Recommended: 1.024 GB • Maximum: 1 GB for the Database Engine Disk: 1-5 GB, depending on software configuration.

Peer-hosted Workgroup Environment

The peer-hosted configuration, deployed for 10 or fewer users, consists of up to 10 computers functioning as clients and one of the 10 computers functioning as the database host as well. All computers contain the RAID client application. The database host also contains the SQL Express 2008 database software that serves as the RAID database. The client computer requirements are less than the minimum standalone workstation requirements described above when not used for database access. All computers must have TCP/IP connectivity through a local area network to the other configured computers. A network speed of 100 Mbps is assumed to meet acceptable performance standards for network-attached clients. The following is a summary of the hardware requirements when operating in a peer-hosted environment. Please refer to the Installation Guide for additional details and caveats.

Component	Requirement
32-bit Peer (client & database server) Computers	
Processor	Processor type: • Pentium III-compatible processor or faster Processor speed: • Minimum: 1.0 GHz • Recommended: 2.0 GHz or faster
Operating System	Windows XP Professional SP2 Windows Server 2003 SP2 Standard Windows Vista Enterprise Windows Server 2008 Standard Server Windows 7 Professional
Memory	RAM: • Minimum: 512 MB • Recommended: 2.048 GB or more • Maximum: Operating system maximum Workstation Disk: 1-5 GB, depending on software configuration. Database Server Disk: 5+ GB, depending on data content.
64-bit Peer (client & database server) Computers	
Processor	Processor type: • Minimum: AMD Opteron, AMD Athlon 64, Intel Xeon with Intel EM64T support, Intel Pentium IV with EM64T support Processor speed: • Minimum: 1.4 GHz • Recommended: 2.0 GHz or faster
Operating System	Windows XP Professional x64 Windows Server 2003 SP2 64-bit x64 Standard Windows Vista Enterprise x64 Windows Server 2008 x64 Standard Windows 7 64-bit x64 Professional
Memory	RAM: • Minimum: 512 MB • Recommended: 1 GB for clients, 2+ GB for database computer • Maximum: Operating system maximum Workstation Disk: 1-5 GB, depending on software configuration. Database Server Disk: 5+ GB, depending on data content.

Server Workgroup Environment

Within the server environment, there is a configuration for internal networked operations which is expected to accommodate up to 50 concurrent users. A network speed of 100 Mbps is assumed to meet minimum performance standards for network-attached clients. The workstations consist of desktop or laptop computers running the RAID client application communicating with a database server over the network. Client computers must meet the configuration requirements for peer client computers above. The database server runs MS SQL Server 2008 (Standard or Enterprise edition) database on a server class Operating System. The following are the minimum hardware requirements for the server machine that hosts the DBMS.

Component	Requirement
32-bit Database Server	
Processor	Processor type: • Pentium III-compatible processor or faster Processor speed: • Minimum: 1.0 GHz • Recommended: 2.0 GHz or faster, 2 cores per instance if supporting more than 10 concurrent users
Operating System	Windows Server 2003 SP2 Standard Windows Server 2008 Standard Server
Memory	RAM: • Minimum: SQL Server 2008 Minimum • Recommended: 2.048 GB per database instance • Maximum: 4 GB, 2 instance maximum Database Server Disk: 5+ GB per instance, depending on data content.
64-bit Database Server	
Processor	Processor type: • Minimum: AMD Opteron, AMD Athlon 64, Intel Xeon with Intel EM64T support, Intel Pentium IV with EM64T support Processor speed: • Minimum: 1.4 GHz • Recommended: 2.0 GHz or faster, 2 cores per instance if supporting more than 10 concurrent users
Operating System	Windows Server 2003 SP2 64-bit x64 Standard Windows Server 2008 x64 Standard
Memory	RAM: • Minimum: SQL Server 2008 Minimum • Recommended: 2.048 GB per database instance • Maximum: 4 GB per database instance Database Server Disk: 5+ GB per instance, depending on data content.

SECTION III: Your Agency's Hardware/Software Configuration

(This section should be filled out by your Technical Point of contact.)
What is your current Hardware Configuration? Check all that apply.

Operating System	Workstation	Database Server	Network Type
Windows XP	☐ 32-bit ☐ 64-bit	☐ 32-bit ☐ 64-bit	☐ Active Directory ☐ TCP
Windows Vista	☐ 32-bit ☐ 64-bit	☐ 32-bit ☐ 64-bit	☐ Active Directory ☐ TCP
Windows 7	☐ 32-bit ☐ 64-bit	☐ 32-bit ☐ 64-bit	☐ Active Directory ☐ TCP
Server 2003	☐ 32-bit ☐ 64-bit	☐ 32-bit ☐ 64-bit	☐ Active Directory ☐ TCP
Server 2008	☐ 32-bit ☐ 64-bit	☐ 32-bit ☐ 64-bit	☐ Active Directory ☐ TCP

*RAID Basic Hardware Requirements are listed in Section II.

Type of RAID License Packaging Requesting:

☐ **Standalone**—the application and Database Management System (DBMS) reside on a single laptop or desktop computer.

☐ **Peer-hosted Workgroup**—the client application resides on a number of laptop or desktop computers, one of which also contains the DBMS to which the other computers connect via a local area network (LAN). Supports up to 10 simultaneous users.

☐ **Server Workgroup**—the client application resides on a number of laptop or desktop computers. The DBMS resides on a dedicated server computer to which the other computers connect via a LAN. Supports 11 and 50 simultaneous users.
** Please indicate the number of required network licenses so the proper number of seats is generated: _____ **

What type of Database will you be using?

☐ SQL Express 2008 (for stand-alone or peer-hosted configuration)

☐ SQL Server 2008 (recommended for server workgroups)

Thank you. If you have any questions, please contact the NDIC Help Desk at (814) 532-4702. This information can be:

- Emailed to NDIC (NDIC.HelpDesk@usdoj.gov), Subject Line: RAID Request
- Mailed to NDIC (National Drug Intelligence Center, Attn: RAID Request, 319 Washington St, 5th Floor, Johnstown, PA, 15901-1622)
- Faxed to (814) 532-5873, Attn: RAID Request

Receiving the RAID application is subject to approval. When approved, NDIC will deliver your RAID application and your Customer Identification number within 10 business days of receiving approval.

The RAID application uses a licensing system. The license strategy will allow you to use the application 30 contiguous days without registration. After the 30th time, you will be required to register your copy of the application in order to continue to use it. We recommend that you register the RAID application prior to the expiration limit.

When you choose to register the application, the license assembly within RAID will generate a ComputerID. Please email the ComputerID to NDIC, along with your assigned Customer Identification number. An NDIC employee will generate and email the activation code to you. Enter the code for continued use of the RAID application. Please note: Because of the complex codes, activation will only occur by email.

INFORMATION SHARING AGREEMENT BETWEEN
THE NATIONAL DRUG INTELLIGENCE CENTER
AND <<Agency Name>>

By signing this document and receiving training on the Real-time Analytical Intelligence Database (RAID), the <<Agency Name>> agrees to share information that will support the strategic intelligence mission of the National Drug Intelligence Center (NDIC). This information will be either in the form of a copy of the RAID databases the <<Agency Name>> created, or synopses of the drug or national security investigations where the RAID application is being used. These synopses can be general, but contain information that would benefit NDIC's strategic analyses and should include:

- Background and history of the investigation
- Targeted organization
- Type and quantity of drugs involved, if applicable
- Impact to U.S. national security, if applicable
- Nationality of principal organization members and size of organization
- Geographic scope of organization
- Trafficking routes (drugs, weapons, etc.) and methods employed
- Organizational vulnerabilities
- Organized crime and/or gang involvement
- Violence associated or perpetrated by organization
- Money laundering techniques employed
- Use of corruption to facilitate or protect organization/activity

Signed _____

Title   _____

Date   _____